ALPHA BOOKS

MAKKAH

ROSIE HANKIN

Evans

EVANS BROTHERS LIMITED

This book is based on *Holy Cities Mecca* by Shahrukh Husain, first published by Evans Brothers Limited in 1993.

Evans Brothers Limited
2A Portman Mansions
Chiltern Street
London W1M 1LE

First published 1999

Typeset by TJ Graphics
Printed in Hong Kong by Wing King Tong

British Library Cataloguing in Publication Data
Hankin, Rosie
Makkah. - (Alpha books)
1. Muslim pilgrims and pilgrimages - Saudi Arabia - Mecca - Juvenile literature
2. Islam - Juvenile literature
3. Mecca (Saudi Arabia) in Islam - Juvenile literature
4. Mecca (Saudi Arabia) - History - Juvenile literature
I. Title
945.6'32

ISBN 0 237 519224

Acknowledgements

Editor: Nicola Barber
Design: David English and TJ Graphics
Consultant: Khadijah Knight
Production: Jenny Mulvanny

Maps: Jillian Luff of Bitmap Graphics

For permission to reproduce copyright material, the author and publishers gratefully acknowledge the following:

Front cover: (main image) Robert Harding Picture Library (top right) Trip

Back cover: Trip

Endpapers: Front - Thousands of pilgrims on their way to the Kaaba during the *Haj* - M. Biber, Robert Harding Picture Library, back - A decorated cover of the Koran - Robert Harding Picture Library

Title page: A decorated copy of the Koran made in the 18th century from Egypt - Trip

p 6 - (top) Tony Souter, Hutchison Library, (bottom) Trip; **p 7** - Trip; **p 8** - (top) Tony Souter, Hutchison Library, (middle) Trip, (bottom) Helene Rogers, Trip; **p 9** - Trip; **p 10** - (top) Trip, (bottom) Trip; **p 11** - Trip; **p 12** - Trip; **p 13** - (top) Trip, (middle) Trip, (bottom) Juliet Highet, Hutchison Library; **p 14** - Robert Harding Picture Library; **p 15** - (top) Robert Harding Picture Library, (bottom) Trip; **p 16** - Trip; **p 17** - Robert Harding Picture Library; **p 18** - Trip; **p 19** - Trip; **p 20** - Trip; **p 21** - Trip; **p 22** - Trip; **p 23** - (top) Trip, (bottom) Bob Turner, Trip; **p 24** - Robert Harding Picture Library; **p 25** - (top) Trip, (middle) Trip, (bottom) Robert Harding Picture Library; **p 26** - (top) Robert Harding Picture Library, (middle) Trip, (bottom) Trip; **p 27** - Trip; **p 28** - Trip; **p 29** - Trip; **p 30** - Trip; **p 31** - Trip; **p 32** - Trip; **p 33** - Trip; **p 34** - Trip; **p 35** - Trip; **p 36** - (top) Trip, (middle) Helene Rogers, Trip, (bottom) Helene Rogers, Trip; **p 37** - Helene Rogers, Trip; **p 38** - (top) Tony Souter, Hutchison Library, (bottom) Trip; **p 39** - Trip; **p 40** - Trip; **p 41** - Trip; **p 42** - (main picture) Robert Harding Picture Library, (inset) John Egan, Hutchison Library; **p 43** - Trip; **p 44** - (left) Hutchison Library, (right) Trip

Contents

Muslims usually say the words 'peace be upon him' after they say the Holy Prophet Muhammad's name. These words have been left out of this book for simplicity.

In the book, the letters CE are used after a date instead of AD appearing before it. CE means 'in the common era' or after the birth of Jesus Christ. So 1200 CE is the same as AD 1200. The letters AH after a date mean 'after the *Hijrah*' when the Prophet Muhammad moved from Makkah and went to Madinah. The *Hijrah* marks the start of the Islamic calendar.

All words in **bold** are explained in the Key words boxes at the end of each chapter.

The importance of Makkah

Five times a day, millions of people all over the world turn towards Makkah to pray. These people are Muslims.They follow the **Prophet** Muhammad.

The Prophet Muhammad was born in Makkah. Today, Makkah lies in the modern country of Saudi Arabia. In the centre of the city is the holy structure called the Ka'bah. Wherever they live, Muslims turn towards the Ka'bah to pray. They pray to Allah (God). The five daily prayers are called *Salah*.

A large **mosque** surrounds the Ka'bah. This area is called the Haram Sharif and the building is The Grand Mosque. Haram Sharif means 'sacred protected area'. At each corner of the Haram Sharif is a tall tower called a minaret. A man called a muezzin stands in a minaret to call Muslims to prayer (*Salah*).

The word Ka'bah means 'cube-shaped'. The Ka'bah is 13 metres tall with a flat roof. It is made of stone. Three pillars inside hold up the roof. The **Qur'an** says that the Prophet Ibrahim and his son Isma'il built the Ka'bah (see page 8). They called it 'Bayt Allah', the House of Allah. It was the first place built for the worship of Allah, the one true God.

▼ The Haram Sharif is in the centre of Makkah.

Key words

Prophet the messenger of God

mosque a Muslim place of worship

Qur'an the holy book of the Muslims

Makkah in the Islamic World

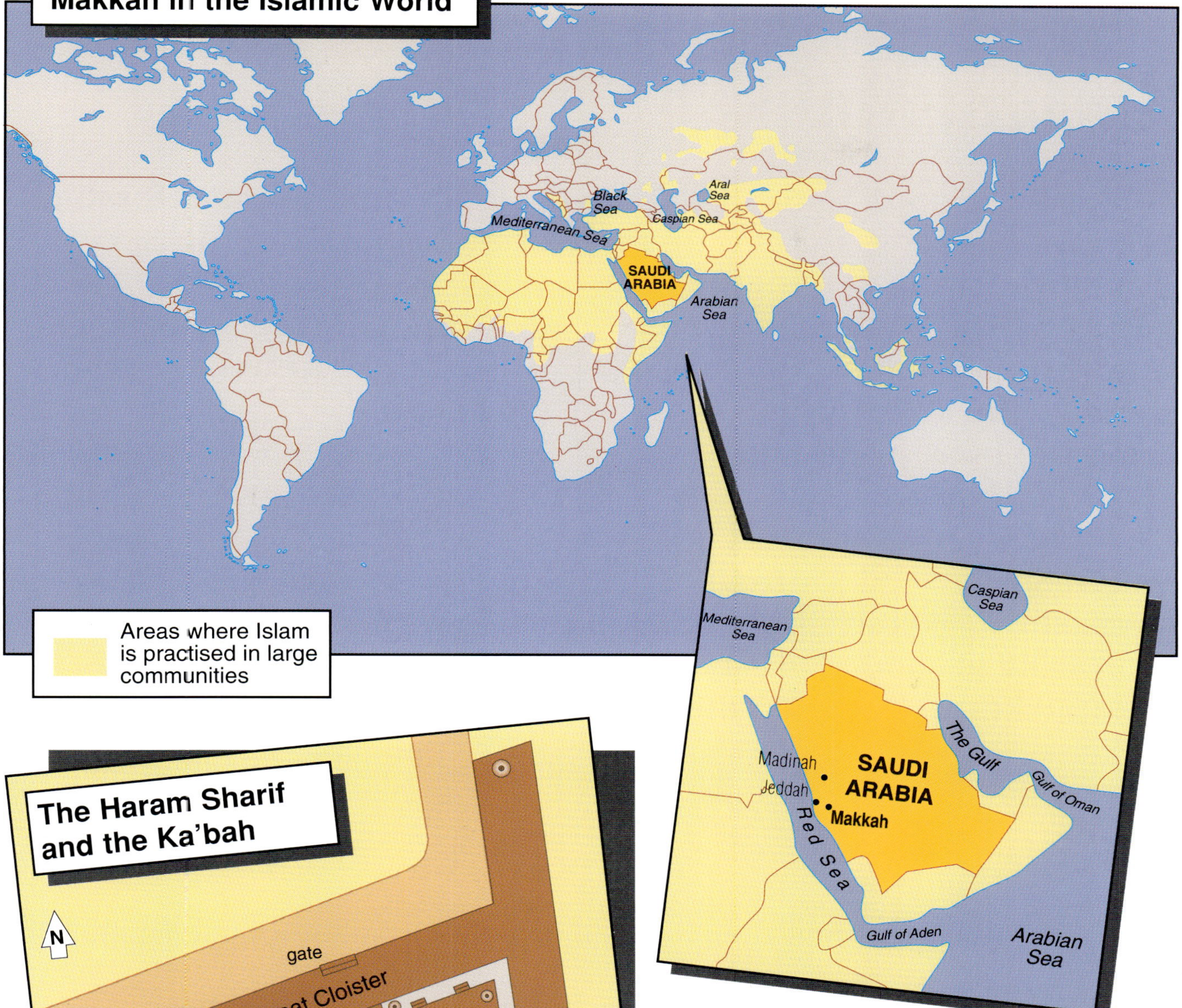

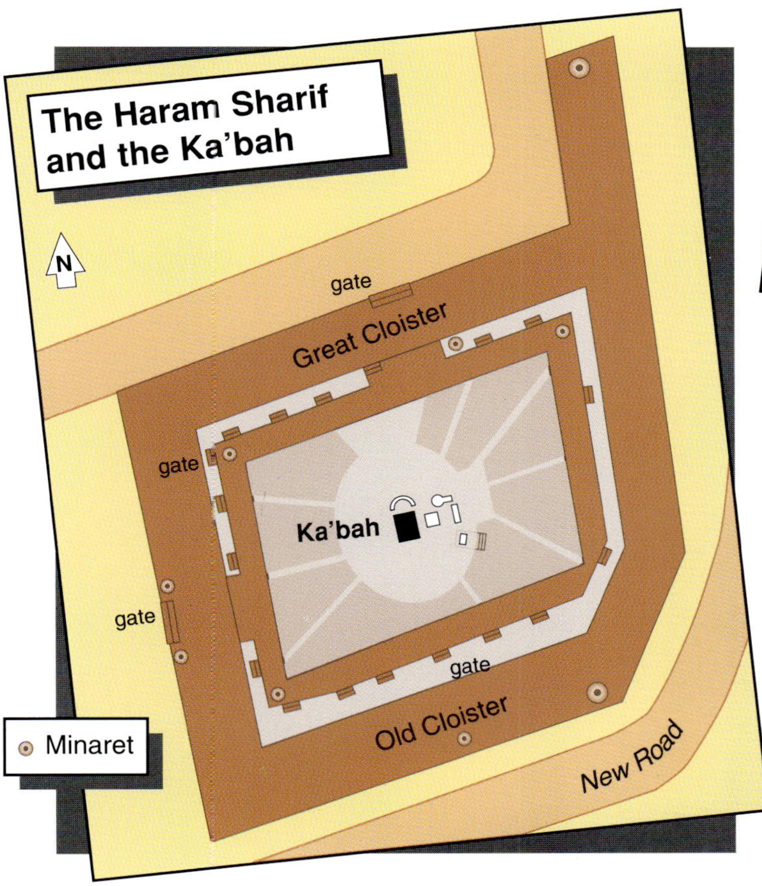

▲ The area around the Ka'bah is called the Haram Sharif.

► These tall towers are called minarets.

Ancient Makkah

Long ago, according to **Islamic** teaching, the Prophet Ibrahim took his wife Hajar and baby son Isma'il into the desert to live. Allah guided them to the Valley of Bakkah. Soon the baby became thirsty. Hajar ran between two hills, Safa and Marwah, looking for water. She prayed for help. Then she saw water bubbling out of the ground. This spring became known as Zamzam.

From time to time, Ibrahim came back to visit his son. When Isma'il was older, he and Ibrahim built the Ka'bah. This was a house to worship the One God.

▲ This is how the Valley of Bakkah would have looked.

▼ A traveller stops at an oasis in the desert.

▲ Market traders at work in Makkah

Isma'il lived by the Ka'bah all his life and worshipped the One God. But after Isma'il died, people began to forget the One God. They filled the Ka'bah with **idols**, and they started to worship many different gods.

As people heard about Zamzam they started to settle near it. This settlement became known as Makkah. Makkah was hidden away in the mountains, in the land of Hijaz. But more and more settlers, travellers and traders came to Makkah. Hundreds of people visited the Ka'bah. Makkah became a crossroads for two trade routes - one connecting Africa and Asia, and the other linking the East with the Mediterranean Sea.

The Spice Route

Traders used camels to transport their goods across the desert. The camels carried spices from the East. These spices were so popular that this road was called the Spice Route. When they got to Makkah, traders had to pay several taxes. They paid a tax on goods sold in Makkah. They also had to pay taxes to carry their goods into and out of the city. The people of Makkah earned a lot of money from the traders.

Pilgrims

Many people came to Makkah to worship at the Ka'bah. These people were called **pilgrims**. Their journey was called a pilgrimage.

While they were in Makkah, the pilgrims spent money in the inns and at the markets. Makkah became a very wealthy city from both the traders and the pilgrims.

▲ A Bedouin woman cooks a meal.

▼ Water pours into a village water tank.

The desert tribes

The people of the land of Hijaz were split into many groups, called tribes. These desert people were called the Bedouin. They lived in the mountains and deserts, and on the outskirts of cities such as Makkah.

Most tribes had the same laws and customs. The most important custom was **hospitality**. In the hot desert people could quickly die of thirst and heat. It was important that travellers could always ask for food, water and shelter. A **host** was expected

▲ Two camels from a **camel caravan**

to allow a guest to stay for at least three days. The host always gave guests plenty to eat and drink.

The different Bedouin tribes were always fighting each other. Their laws told them how to fight, how to treat their prisoners and how to punish different crimes.

The Bedouin were **nomadic.** This means that they travelled from place to place with their herds of sheep and goats. Their lives were hard. Sometimes they raided towns and stole food and other goods. Others worked as caravan guides or as guards.

The people of Makkah

Unlike the Bedouin, the people of Makkah were settled and rich. In the years before the birth of the Prophet Muhammad, the tribe of Quraysh was the most important in Makkah. Its chief,

▼ Camel harnesses inside a Bedouin tent

Abdul Muttalib, was the head of the council of elders. This council ruled the city.

Some women played an important part in life in Makkah. Most of these women worked in business or helped to run the city. One woman merchant, Khadijah, married the Prophet Muhammad.

The culture of the desert

Although the people of Makkah loved their city, they did not forget that they were once nomads. Some rich families in Makkah sent their children to live with the Bedouin. The children grew up in Bedouin families and learned their ways.

These children became skilled at riding and fighting, and they learned about honour, loyalty and bravery. They learned about the desert and how to travel through it. They also learned another important Bedouin art – making up and speaking poetry. Bedouin poems told stories of war, love and history.

Key words

Islamic describes the Muslim religion, Islam

idol a statue which people worship as if it were a god

pilgrim someone who goes on a special journey to a holy place

hospitality kindness in welcoming strangers and guests

host a person who looks after a guest

nomadic moving from place to place

camel caravan a group of camels travelling together

Think and do

1. Life in the desert was hard. How did the Bedouin help each other?
2. In the picture on page 11 you can see inside a Bedouin tent. You could try making your own designs for striped rugs and tent material.

The messenger

In the years before the Prophet Muhammad was born, Makkah was a very rich place. The spice trade was doing well. The camel caravans took leather, dried fruit, silver and gold, perfumes and medicines from Makkah. The caravans returned with silk, slaves, weapons, cereals and oils.

People in other countries wanted a share in the riches of Makkah. The emperors of Byzantine and Persia and the king of **Abyssinia** (Ethiopia) worried that the tribes of Hijaz would join together and attack them. So they made sure the

▲ A display of gold jewellery in a shop

◄ Raisins drying

▼ Herbs and spices for sale in a market

▲ An early Christian church in Abyssinia

Bedouin tribes were always fighting each other.

In 570 CE, the Abyssinian king of Yemen attacked Makkah. His name was Abraha and he was a Christian. Abraha built a church in Yemen. He wanted pilgrims to go to his church and not to the Ka'bah. So he decided to destroy the Ka'bah.

Abraha crossed the desert with his soldiers and an elephant. He ordered his soldiers to surround Makkah. Then he told the people of Makkah to surrender. When they refused Abraha ordered his men and the elephant to attack the city.

At that moment, swarms of small birds filled the sky and threw stones on to Abraha's army. The elephant collapsed. Abraha was frightened by this **miracle** from heaven and fled. The people of Makkah named this the Year of the Elephant.

The most precious gift

Around this time, a woman called Amina was expecting a baby. Amina belonged to the Quraysh tribe. Amina's husband, Abdullah, was the son of Abdul Muttalib (see page 12). Sadly, Abdullah died before the baby was born.

In about 570 CE, Amina gave birth to a boy. She named him Muhammad. Following the custom, Amina gave

Muhammad to a Bedouin woman (see page 12). Muhammad stayed in the desert with the woman, called Halima, for four years. He learned about Bedouin life, especially about hospitality.

Amina died when Muhammad was six. He was looked after by his grandfather, and then by his uncle, Abu Talib, who loved and protected him.

▲ Young boys herd their flocks of sheep and goats.

The Holy Prophet

Muhammad grew up to be a kind and honest boy. People gave him the nickname Al-Amin, which means 'The Truthful'. At first, Muhammad worked for his uncle. Later, he worked for a woman called Khadijah. Muhammad and Khadijah married and they had many children. Their sons died, but their four daughters all grew up and got married. One of them, Fatima, married Ali, the son of Abu Talib.

▲ A Bedouin boy with his father

Key words

Abyssinia the old name for Ethiopia

miracle a wonderful and surprising event which people believe is caused by God

The message

In 612 CE, when Muhammad was about 40, he often went to a cave on Mount Hira, just outside Makkah. Muhammad went there to be by himself and to think. One day, the Angel Jibril appeared to him. Jibril had a message from Allah. Muhammad was to tell the people that there was only one God, Allah, and that they should worship only Allah. From this time, Muhammad became Allah's messenger.

Allah gave many messages to Muhammad through the Angel Jibril. They described Allah as the Supreme Power who was 'all merciful' and 'all forgiving'. The angel told Muhammad about the prophets of the past, such as Musa (Moses), Ibrahim (Abraham) and Isa (Jesus). All of these prophets lived in Jerusalem.

◀ Muhammad went to Mount Hira (at the back of the picture) to be alone and think.

Difficult times

The first people to accept Muhammad's message were his wife Khadijah and his cousin Ali. Believers became known as Muslims. Muslim means someone who is willing to obey Allah. Muslims declare their faith with these words, called the ***Shahadah***:

'There is no god except Allah, Muhammad is the Messenger of Allah.'

Some people, such as Muhammad's uncle, Abu Talib, respected Muhammad but did not accept his message. But most wealthy people in Makkah hated Muhammad because he told them that

▲ The city of Jerusalem, where the three prophets Musa, Ibrahim and Isa once lived

their gods were false. They said that if people believed Muhammad, the Ka'bah would lose its importance. Pilgrims would stop coming to Makkah and the city would be less rich.

Khadijah died, followed soon after by Muhammad's uncle, Abu Talib. Muhammad grieved deeply. He wanted to leave Makkah, and his life was always in danger. Some people in the neighbouring city of Yathrib asked Muhammad to come to their city. So in 622 CE, Muhammad moved to Yathrib with his friend Abu Bakr. This move is called the ***Hijrah***, or 'migration'. Muslims use the date of the *Hijrah* as the starting point of their calendar.

After Muhammad arrived in Yathrib, the city was renamed 'Madinatu'n-Nabi' (City of the Prophet), or Madinah.

Key words

Shahadah The declaration of faith made by Muslims: 'There is no God except Allah, Muhammad is the Messenger of Allah.'

Hijrah The migration of Muhammad from Makkah to Madinah in 622 CE.

Madinah, City of the Prophet

The climate of Madinah was pleasant although the summers were hot. There was plenty of water. Date palms and other fruit trees grew in the good soil. Farmers worked on the land around the city. It was very different from the dry, mountainous land around Makkah.

When Muhammad arrived in Madinah, many people offered him hospitality and land. But the Prophet did not want to be a burden to other people. He said he would build his own house where his camel stopped. The people followed Muhammad and his camel until the animal stopped. Muhammad bought the land and he and his companions began to build. As they worked they sang a song:

'If we sit down when the
Prophet works
It may be said that we have
been lazy.'

In Madinah

Muhammad built his house around a large, open courtyard. Muhammad met his visitors in this courtyard.

▼ Ancient Madinah (left) and Makkah (right) in a decorated book

Top: These men are building a house using local stone

Below: This is the Mosque of the Prophet in Madinah.

◀ This mosque in El Gassim is made from baked clay.

He also led the *Salah* (prayers) five times a day. The homeless and travellers were always welcome, even when Muhammad had little food. Muhammad married Aishah, Abu Bakr's young daughter.

At first Muslims prayed facing Jerusalem. Then the angel told Muhammad that they should face the Ka'bah. The angel said that all Muslims should go to the Ka'bah for *Hajj* (pilgrimage) at least once in their lives (see pages 28-33).

During 623 CE, Allah sent a

▲ The city of Madinah as it is today

message to Muhammad through the Angel Jibril to instruct all Muslims to fast during the Islamic month of Ramadan. The first day of the following month, Shawal, would be set aside for a feast called *Id-ul-Fitr* (see page 37).

Back to Makkah

Islam became more and more popular. The people of Makkah did not like this. There was a lot of fighting between them and the Muslims. Two great battles were fought at Badr in 624 CE and at Uhud in 625 CE.

In 628 CE, Allah told Muhammad that he would return to Makkah. So Muhammad and his followers travelled to Makkah. The people of Makkah made an agreement with Muhammad. The agreement said that the Muslims could return to Makkah each year on pilgrimage. But the people of Makkah broke this agreement. So Muhammad organised an army to enter Makkah. The people of Makkah surrendered without fighting. At the Ka'bah, Muhammad told the city elders that he had won Makkah for the Muslims through the Grace of Allah.

Islam unites Makkah

Muhammad destroyed all the idols in the Ka'bah. Soon all the different tribes of Makkah

▲ Pilgrims travel to Makkah to take part in the *Hajj.*

accepted Islam. Makkah became the holiest city of Islam.

After years of spreading the message of Islam, Muhammad was tired and ill. He developed a fever and on the 12th day of the Islamic month Rabi-al-Awwal 632 CE Muhammad died. He was buried at his home in Madinah. This is now the Mosque of the Prophet (see page 19).

The Five Pillars of Islam

The Five Pillars of Islam are rules that all Muslims must obey:

All Muslims must proclaim, 'There is no god except Allah, Muhammad is the Messenger of Allah'.
All Muslims should perform five sets of salah *each day.*
All Muslims should fast during the month of Ramadan, eating and drinking nothing before dawn until sunset.
All Muslims should give zakah (charity) equal to 2.5 per cent of their wealth after all outgoings.
All Muslims should make a pilgrimage to Makkah at least once in their lifetime.

After the death of the Holy Prophet, his friend Abu Bakr led the Muslims. He was the first ***Khalifah***. He was followed by Umar, then Uthman, and eventually Ali.

The Holy Qur'an

The word Qur'an means 'that which is read or recited'. Every

▲ This is the oldest handwritten Qur'an, made in 640 CE.

◀ This is the Qur'an printing press in Madinah.

year, during the month of Ramadan, Muhammad had spoken out loud to the Angel Jibril all the messages received from Allah. Many of his companions also remembered the complete message. Other people wrote it down. But people began to make copies in different dialects which altered the meaning. So Uthman collected together all the copies. Then he made sure that correct copies were made, with the message exactly as the Angel Jibril revealed it to the Prophet Muhammad. These are the words of the Muslim holy book, the Qur'an.

Key words

***Khalifah* (caliph)** means successor, or custodian.

The spread of Islam

After the death of Muhammad, Islam spread quickly outside Arabia. Under the leadership of Umar, the Muslims conquered Iraq, Jerusalem, Persia (now Iran) and Egypt.

Uthman became *Khalifah* in 644 CE. Ali followed him as *Khalifah*. Ali was the son-in-law of the Prophet Muhammad. He died in 661 CE. Some Muslims believed that only **descendants** of the Prophet Muhammad could be *Khalifah*. They became known as the Shi'at Ali (Party of Ali), or Shi'ah for short. Other Muslims said they wanted to elect their leader. They became known as Sunni Muslims.

After Ali, the Umayyad **dynasty** (family) took over the ***Khilafah***. They moved their capital to Damascus in Syria. Soon the Islamic Empire stretched from Spain in the

▼ Inside the mosque at Cordoba, Spain (see page 24)

▲ The dome and minaret of a mosque in Baghdad, Iraq

▲ Once a year, Muslim rulers sent a beautiful camel seat as a gift to Makkah.

west (see picture page 23) to Central Asia in the east.

Although Arabia was no longer the political centre of the empire, it was important because of the holy cities, Makkah and Madinah. Makkah was always the most holy city of Islam, and pilgrims came from far and wide to the city.

In 750 CE the Abbasid dynasty took over the *Khilafah* from the Umayyads. The Abbasids moved their capital to Baghdad in Iraq. From there they conquered more areas of Asia, reaching India.

The Ottomans originally came from Turkey. They established one of the greatest Muslim empires. In 1453 CE they captured Constantinople and made it their capital. They renamed it Istanbul. Then they conquered most of the Middle East, Egypt and the Hijaz.

The Ottoman **sultan** (leader) forced the last Abbasid *Khalifah* to hand over the title. The Ottomans ruled Hijaz for 400 years. The sultans had great respect for Makkah. Under their protection, pilgrims flocked to Makkah from the Middle East and Asia, and even from Indonesia.

The Ottoman Empire finally ended when the sultans joined the Germans in World War I (1914-18). By the end of the war, the British and French had taken over many of the lands once ruled by the Ottomans.

Recent history

In 1932 Hijaz became part of a new country, Saudi Arabia. Saudi Arabia was named after its leader, Abd al-Aziz Ibn Saud. The present ruler of Saudi Arabia is Fahd Ibn Abdul Aziz. He took the title 'Custodian of the Sacred Places'. The sacred places are Makkah and Madinah. He has made many improvements to the religious sites in and around Makkah.

▲ Inside the royal tent at the races in Saudi Arabia

► King Fahd Ibn Abdul Aziz

▼ The Blue Mosque in Istanbul, Turkey

Key words

descendants someone's descendants are later generations who are related to them.

dynasty a succession of rulers who all come from the same family.

Khilafah the institution (tradition) of the *Khalifah*.

sultan the name for a leader in some Muslim countries.

Modern Makkah

Saudi Arabia has very rich oil reserves. In the 1970s, the price of oil went up and Saudi Arabia sold a lot of oil. Because of this, Saudi Arabia became very rich. The Saudi Arabians used some of this money to put up new buildings in Makkah.

Every year, millions of pilgrims go to Makkah. Some pilgrims are on a pilgrimage called *Umrah*, which they can make at any time of the year. Many come for the *Hajj*, which happens once every year (see page 28). Over two million pilgrims travel to Makkah for the *Hajj*.

▼ Building work in Saudi Arabia started in the 1970s.

Top: Oil pipes in Saudi Arabia

▲ Modern buildings surround the Haram Sharif.

People in Makkah decided to make more space for the pilgrims. In the middle of the city, buildings were pulled down and whole areas were cleared. People moved out from the centre to new homes on the outskirts of the city. There were new motorways and roads, hospitals and health centres.

Public services

One problem in Makkah was that fresh water was often in short supply. So the government built huge new **desalination** plants on the Red Sea. A desalination plant takes out salt from sea water to make fresh water. This water is safe for people to drink. Today, the desalination plants provide Makkah with plenty of fresh drinking water.

Preparing for the *Hajj*

The *Hajj* affects everyone in Makkah. The people of Makkah have to hand their city over to the pilgrims and offer them all the help they can. For the pilgrims, their visit to Makkah is a dream come true. The roads are kept clear for them as they travel into the city. The people of Makkah must park their cars outside the city and use public transport.

Of course, the *Hajj* is good for business. The hotels are full of pilgrims. The pilgrims need food and drink, so the markets are well stocked. Street sellers are everywhere. The pilgrims buy prayer beads, prayer mats and small Qur'ans to use on the *Hajj*. Local people work as guides to lead the pilgrims through the *Hajj* in the correct way. They come from families who have done this job for many years.

There is always a feeling of excitement in Makkah as the pilgrimage month of Dhul-Hijjah draws near.

▲ *Hajj* guides lead pilgrims to a holy site.

▼ Tents for pilgrims are fire-proofed for safety.

Key words

desalination the process of removing salt from something, for example sea water.

City of grace

As the month of the *Hajj* approaches, pilgrims start to arrive in Saudi Arabia. Once, the journey could take several years. Today, the journey usually takes only a few days or even hours. Many pilgrims fly to Jeddah airport. Air-conditioned cars and coaches take the pilgrims from Jeddah airport to Makkah.

The *Hajj* begins

The pilgrims dress in white for the *Hajj*. As they approach the Haram Sharif (see page 6) they chant *'Labbaika, Allah humma labbaik'*, which

▼ A pilgrim sells jewellery to help pay for his *Hajj*.

▲ Pilgrims enter the Haram Sharif.

means 'Here I am, Oh Allah, at your service.' Inside the Haram Sharif is the Ka'bah.

The *Kiswa*

The Ka'bah is covered by a black cloth called the ***Kiswa***. The *Kiswa* is covered in golden embroidery. The embroidery spells out the *Shahadah*:

'There is no god except Allah, Muhammad is the Messenger of Allah.'

The *Kiswa* is made in Makkah. It measures 232 square metres and weighs two tonnes.

On the 25th of Dhul-Qad'ah, the month before Dhul-Hijjah, there is a special ceremony to remove the old *Kiswa*. The 'Custodian of the Sacred Places' (see page 25), who is the king of the day, cleans the

Far left: Weaving the cloth for the *Kiswa*

◄ Embroidering the *Kiswa*

inside the of Ka'bah. The new *Kiswa* is placed over the Ka'bah on the 27th of Dhul-Hijjah.

The first step of the *Hajj*

The first step of the *Hajj* is to circle the Ka'bah. Pilgrims walk round the Ka'bah seven times, moving anti-clockwise. This is called *Tawaf*. They start from the black stone in the corner of the Ka'bah.

The Maqam Ibrahim

The Maqam Ibrahim is a small glass case. Inside the Maqam Ibrahim is a boulder on a

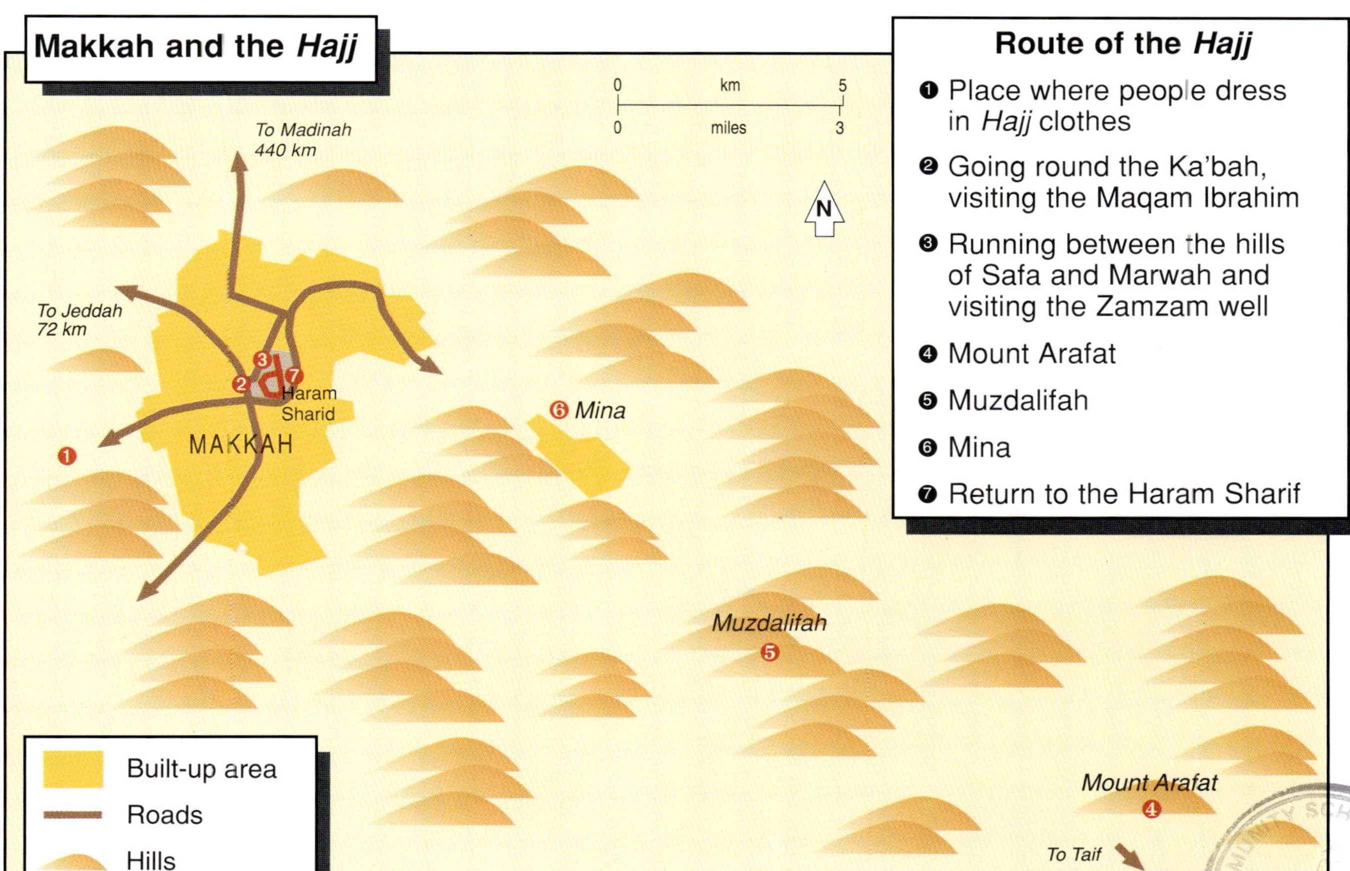

▲ Pilgrims touch the Ka'bah.

marble stand. This is the boulder that Ibrahim stood on to build the Ka'bah (see page 8). The pilgrims say prayers at the Maqam Ibrahim.

Safa and Marwah
Beyond the clear space around the Ka'bah was an area filled with shops and traffic. This separated the Ka'bah from the strip of desert where Hajar

▼ The Maqam Ibrahim

looked for water for baby Isma'il (see page 8). The shops are no longer there and this area is now part of the Haram Sharif. Pilgrims walk seven times between the hills of Safa and Marwah – just as Hajar did.

Some pilgrims go on to drink some water from the Zamzam well. Until recently a large building covered the well. Now the building has gone and a marble staircase leads down to the well.

▲ Pilgrims walk seven times between Safa and Marwah.

Mount Arafat
On the ninth day of Dhul-Hijjah pilgrims gather on the wide plain beneath Mount Arafat. Mount Arafat is about 25 kilometres east of Makkah. Part of Mount Arafat is called the Mount of Mercy. This is where the Prophet Muhammad

Some pilgrims travel on foot (**above**), but most pilgrims use *Hajj* buses.

talked to his followers.

Pilgrims used to travel to Arafat on foot or by camel. Now most go by coach. The pilgrims stay in tents on the plain of Arafat. The whole plain is covered with thousands of tents.

In the afternoon, the pilgrims get as close as they can to the place where the Prophet Muhammad gave his farewell speech. They stand in the hot sun and worship Allah, praying and asking for forgiveness. Then in the early evening they set out for Muzdalifah.

Muzdalifah

The pilgrims spend the night in Muzdalifah. This is halfway between Arafat and Mina. The moon is nearly full and lights the desert. Many pilgrims pray through the night. They also collect small stones from the ground at Muzdalifah. Next morning they leave for Mina.

▲ Thousands of tents at Mount Arafat

▲ This is the mosque at Arafat.

Mina

Mina is on the way back to Makkah. It is a small town of stone houses surrounded by cliffs. The pilgrims throw their stones at three pillars. The pillars stand for devils. The pilgrims throw their stones to show that they reject these devils. For three days the pilgrims return to Mina to stone the pillars.

On the tenth day of Dhul-Hijjah the pilgrims celebrate *Id-ul-Adha*. They buy a sheep, goat or camel. The animal is killed as an offering to Allah. Some of the meat is given to the poor. This reminds pilgrims that Ibrahim was willing to sacrifice his son at Allah's command. The killing of the sheep, goats and camels takes place according to Islamic laws.

Many male pilgrims have the hair shaved from their heads. Female pilgrims do not have to shave their heads, but they must cut off at least 2.5 centimetres of hair.

The pilgrims return to Makkah. They walk around the Ka'bah again for another seven times. Then they pray in the Haram Sharif. Around 500,000 people can fit into the Haram

▲ Pilgrims collect stones at Muzdalifah.

Pilgrims pray at Mina. ►

▲ Thousands of pilgrims pray at the Ka'bah.

Sharif at any one time.

Many pilgrims visit Madinah after the *Hajj*. In Madinah they go to pray in the Mosque of the Prophet, where the Prophet Muhammad is buried (see page 21).

Key words

Kiswa The cloth that is placed over the Ka'bah.

Think and do

1. Describe the *Hajj* in your own words. Imagine you are a pilgrim. How do you feel?

Life in Makkah

Work and prayer

Each day, before dawn, the muezzin (crier) calls the people of Makkah to prayer. This call to prayer is called the *Adhan*. People get up and wash themselves. This is called *wudu*. Men may go to one of the mosques. Women often pray at home.

Five times each day, the city comes to a stop. Everyone spends a few minutes in prayer. They pray anywhere – in offices, shops and even on the pavement.

Eating and relaxing

Lunch is the main meal in Makkah. People eat meat, rice and vegetables. They love salad, too. Puddings are cooling and milky. They are often flavoured with rose water. Arab pastries are crisp, flaky and delicious. They often contain pistachio nuts and are soaked in syrup. Guests are always welcome at a meal.

Midday is very hot. Most people stay at home. Some sleep, others sit and chat.

◄ Muezzins call from tall minarets.

▼ Praying at home on a prayer mat

► A basket of fresh fruit

▼ Dishes of snacks

◄ Shopping in the market

▲ Drinking tea in the shade

In the afternoon the city comes alive again. The shops open at 5 p.m. and close late at night. Families go out to the parks and playgrounds. At weekends they might go to the mountains. Arafat is popular for evening picnics.

The people of Makkah

The people of Makkah come from many different places. Many have a connection with the oldest tribes of Hijaz. Some were visitors who decided to stay. There are Muslims from Africa, India, Indonesia, Central Asia, Afghanistan and Russia. Although these people come from various countries they are all united by their Islamic beliefs.

Family life is important. Children must respect and honour their parents. Often grandparents, uncles, aunts and cousins all live together as a family. Today, many younger people often choose to live in their own apartments. But when parents become old, their children look after them.

▲ The people of Makkah come from many countries.

Festivals

Islamic festivals usually celebrate an event that took place in or around Makkah. The people of Makkah are proud that their city is remembered all over the world.

Ramadan

Ramadan is one of the holiest months in the Islamic calendar. It was when the Prophet Muhammad first received the

▲ Beating drums outside a mosque in Morocco during *Laylat-ul-Qadr*

▼ Shopping at night during Ramadan

▲ Saudi Arabians celebrate with dancing.

message of Allah from the Angel Jibril. During Ramadan, Muslims do not eat or drink from before sunrise until sunset. They pray and try to be especially good.

Laylat-ul-Qadr (the Night of Power) marks the time when the Qur'an was first revealed to Muhammad. Muslims believe that it was on one of the last ten nights of Ramadan.

Makkah changes into a night city during Ramadan. People break their fast then stay up with their friends. The shops stay open all night. Just before dawn people have a meal. Then they say their morning prayers and sleep for a while.

Id-ul-Fitr

As Ramadan draws to a close,

people look for the thin crescent moon that shows a new month is beginning. When it is, the next day is *Id-ul-Fitr*. In Makkah religious officials announce the sighting of the new moon. This is so Muslims all over the world can celebrate *Id* on the same day.

Id begins with prayers in the mosque. Then people visit friends and relatives. They feast all day. Everyone has dates and milk. Children get gifts of money and sweets.

Id-ul-Adha

Id-ul-Adha is the most important holy festival (see page 32). It is the feast of the sacrifice. It happens towards the end of the *Hajj*.

▲ These sheep are being taken to Saudi Arabia for *Id-ul-Fitr.*

Key words

Ramadan The ninth month of the Islamic calendar, during which Muslims fast from just before dawn until sunset.

Think and do

1. Try painting your own picture of a Muslim festival.

These are paintings of festivals by Saudi children.

A focus for Muslims

Since the beginning of Islam, Makkah has been an important centre for Islamic study. Students from all over the world came to Makkah to learn about Islamic law. They worked in groups led by a scholar. They met in the buildings of the Haram Sharif As numbers increased, the scholars opened their homes to the students. These schools were called the *katatib*. Students learned reading, writing, grammar and Islamic studies. The tradition still continues.

Today, Makkah has several schools and universities. Islamic studies are an important part of education. Children start school when they are six. They learn about Islam and how it affects their lives. Older students study at a College of **Shari'ah** and Islamic Studies. These are part of the Ummul Qura University. Many students stay on in Makkah, to be near the Haram Sharif.

Islam is such an important part of life in Saudi Arabia that the *Shahadah* (see page 16)

▲ Students studying science in a classroom

▲ Students enjoy sport.

appears on the national flag. The flag flies at all ports and borders. It is never flown at half-mast (halfway down the flagpole) because of its holy message.

Saudi rulers are proud of Makkah. They have worked hard to make it a model city. They feel this is their duty because Makkah is the focus for Muslims across the whole world.

▲ The flag and emblem of Saudi Arabia

Key words

Shari'ah Islamic law based on the Qur'an and the Sunnah.

Think and do

1. Describe why Makkah is so important to Saudi Arabia and to the rest of the Islamic world.

Art and buildings

Geometric shapes

Islamic art uses a lot of **geometric** shapes and patterns. A geometric shape is made out of regular lines and shapes such as triangles, circles and squares. Islamic artists also make beautiful patterns with the shapes of flowers and leaves.

For centuries, students in Makkah have studied **astronomy** and mathematics. These subjects were very important for Muslims. Many Muslim artists used the patterns of the stars as inspiration for their designs.

▲ Patterned carpets and plasterwork in a Saudi house

◀ A Bedouin tent cloth

▼ A beautiful patterned carpet

Muslim artists must not use human figures in their designs. This goes back to the time when there were idols of many gods in the Ka'bah (see page 9). The followers of Muhammad thought that pictures of humans might encourage people to go back to worshipping many gods. So the walls of mosques and other buildings are covered with colourful patterned tiles.

Calligraphy

Beautiful writing is called **calligraphy**. Muslims use calligraphy to decorate copies of the Qur'an. They also use it to make elaborate patterns and shapes on the walls of mosques.

The words for a beautiful piece of calligraphy are usually taken from the Qur'an. The words are written or carved with coils and curls of the pen. Calligraphers use the words to form the shapes of ships, minarets, birds and animals.

Mosques

Mosques in Makkah, like mosques all over the world, are modelled on the Prophet Muhammad's house. There is a courtyard surrounded by arcades. There is often a fountain or a well in the courtyard where people can wash before going to pray. In the wall closest to Makkah, there is an alcove in the wall, called the *mihrab*. The *mihrab* faces in the direction of the Ka'bah. It shows Muslims which way to face when they pray. The *mihrab* is often decorated with beautiful patterns and designs.

The *minbar* is a raised platform. This is where the *imam* (prayer leader) stands to read from the Qur'an and speak to the worshippers.

Some mosques also have a tall tower called a minaret. This is where the muezzin stands to call Muslims to prayer.

Everyone must take their shoes off before entering a mosque, so there are always rows of shoes at the doors.

▲ This doorway is decorated with calligraphy.

▼ This calligraphy forms a shape called an **arabesque**.

▲ The mosque in Brunei, Southeast Asia. You can see the tall minaret on the left-hand side. The dome is covered in gold.

▲ A tile panel in Topkapi Palace, Istanbul.

Key words

geometric shapes made up of triangles, squares and circles.

astronomy the study of the stars and planets.

calligraphy the art of beautful handwriting.

arabesque a decorative shape made up of leaf, flower or geometric designs.

Changes in Makkah

The rest of Makkah is very different from the Haram Sharif. The city was once built in circles around the Ka'bah. The buildings were so close that their shadows met at dawn and dusk. There was hardly any space for prayer around the Ka'bah.

The buildings shaded people from the hot sun. Markets were covered to keep people cool. The houses had thick stone walls and narrow windows to shut out the heat.

▲ Houses on the outskirts of Makkah

Houses and apartments

People in the same family liked to live near each other. So as a family grew, new houses were built next to the old family home. Rich families live in large mansions. People built their houses around a large, open courtyard.

In the 1970s, Saudi Arabia became rich from oil (see pages 26-7). The government used some of the money to rebuild Makkah. Poeple pulled down many beautiful old buildings. They built new houses and apartment blocks instead. These modern buildings have thin walls and large doors and windows. They are not well suited to the climate but most people have air-conditioning in their homes. This keeps them cool.

▼ Old, narrow lanes in Makkah. In the background is a modern tower block.

Beautiful decoration and plasterwork on Saudi buildings.

Markets and gardens

Makkah has two large parks, the Zahir Gardens and the Masfalah Gardens. Like other modern cities, there are shopping arcades and supermarkets. But the traditional markets are still popular.

Conservation

Many people now think that the original design of Makkah was better in many ways than the modern one. They are now trying to preserve the older buildings. There will still be many more changes in this remarkable city. But it will always be the most holy city for millions of Muslims.

▼ A city garden in Makkah

Important events

CE (AD)

about 571 Muhammad is born.

609 Muhammad receives messages on Mount Hira. His followers know he is the Prophet of Allah.

622 The Holy Prophet moves to Madinah in the *Hijrah*. This is counted as year 1 in the Islamic calendar.

624 The Muslim army defeats people of Makkah at Badr.

627 The Muslim army pushes back Makkah's army at Madinah.

628 Muhammad signs treaty allowing a *Hajj* in 629 CE.

630 The Muslim army captures Makkah.

632 Muhammad dies.

632-61 The first four successors to the leadership role of the Prophet Muhammad are Abu Bakr, Umar, Uthman and Ali. They are known as the Rightly Guided *Khalifas*.
Prayer space around the Ka'bah is increased. Makkah becomes the capital of Arabia.

650 The Qur'an is collated and remains unchanged today.

661 The last of the four Rightly Guided *Khalifas* is killed.

661-750 The Umayyad *Khilafah* dominates the Muslim world.

711-15 North African Muslims advance into Spain.

750-1100 The Abbasid *Khilafah* of Baghdad takes over from the Umayyads.

968-1171 Muslim culture flourishes under the Egyptian Fatimid ruling dynasty.

1453 The Ottoman Empire is founded and conquers Constantinople (Istanbul).

1517 The Ottomans take over Egypt and Hijaz.

1585 The Ottoman Empire declines.

1803 Muhammad Wahhab and followers, under Muhammad Ibn Saud, capture Makkah.

1916 Muslim Arabs take over Makkah from the Ottomans.

1919 Makkah is no longer capital of Arabia.

1919-24 Abdul Aziz Ibn Saud wins a battle in Hijaz and takes Makkah.

1926 Ibn Saud is made king of Hijaz.

1932 The Hijaz kingdom becomes part of Saudi Arabia.

1965 The Maqam Ibrahim is made smaller and enclosed. The Zamzam well is opened up. The Ottoman buildings at the Haram Sharif are greatly extended and enlarged.

Index